Living and Nonliving in the
Ocean

Rebecca Rissman

Heinemann
LIBRARY

Chicago, Illinois

© 2014 Heinemann Library
an imprint of Capstone Global Library, LLC
Chicago, Illinois

To contact Capstone Global Library please phone
800-747-4992, or visit our website
www.capstonepub.com

Edited by Daniel Nunn, Rebecca Rissman, and
Catherine Veitch
Designed by Cynthia Della-Rovere
Picture research by Tracy Cummins
Production by Sophia Argyris
Originated by Capstone Global Library Ltd

ISBN 978-1-4109-5381-0 (hc)
ISBN 978-1-4109-5388-9 (pb)

Library of Congress Cataloging-in-Publication Data
Rissman, Rebecca.
 Living and nonliving in the ocean / Rebecca Rissman.—
1st ed.
     p. cm.—(Is it living or nonliving?)
 Includes bibliographical references and index.
 ISBN 978-1-4109-5381-0 (hb)—ISBN 978-1-4109-5388-
9 (pb) 1. Marine ecology—Juvenile literature. 2. Marine
animals—Juvenile literature. 3. Marine plants—Juvenile
literature. I. Title.

 QH541.5.S3R57 2013
 577.7—dc23   2012046868

Printed and bound in the USA.
009956RP

Image Credits
Alamy: Reinhard Dirscherl, cover, 15; Getty Images:
microgen, 9, Norbert Probst, 18, Steven Trainoff Ph.D, 20;
Science Source: Andrew J. Martinez, 10; Shutterstock:
A Cotton Photo, 8, Alberto Pérez Veiga, 4, Anna segeren,
16, cbpix, 6, 23 (top), designsstock, 17, 23 (bottom
middle), Ekaterina Lin, 19, Galyna Andrushko, 23 (bottom),
Levent Konuk, 14, Pichugin Dmitry, 12, Rich Carey, 5, 7,
trekandshoot, 1, Volodymyr Goinyk, 22, whitewizzard,
back cover, 13, worldswildlifewonders, 21, Marevision/age
fotostock, 11, 23 (top middle)

We would like to thank Michael Bright and Nancy Harris for
their invaluable help in the preparation of this book.

Some words are in bold, **like this**.
You can find them in the glossary on page 23.

Contents

What Is an Ocean?

An ocean is a very large body of water.

Oceans are full of salt water.

Different types of plants and animals live in the oceans.
There are **nonliving** things in the oceans too.

What Are Living Things?

Living things are alive. Living things need air and **sunlight**. Living things move on their own.

Living things need food and water.

Living things grow and change.

What Are Nonliving Things?

Nonliving things are not alive. Nonliving things do not need air and **sunlight**.

Nonliving things do not need food or water.

Nonliving things do not move on their own.

Nonliving things do not grow and change on their own.

Is a Lobster Living or Nonliving?

A **lobster** needs food and water.

A lobster moves on its own.

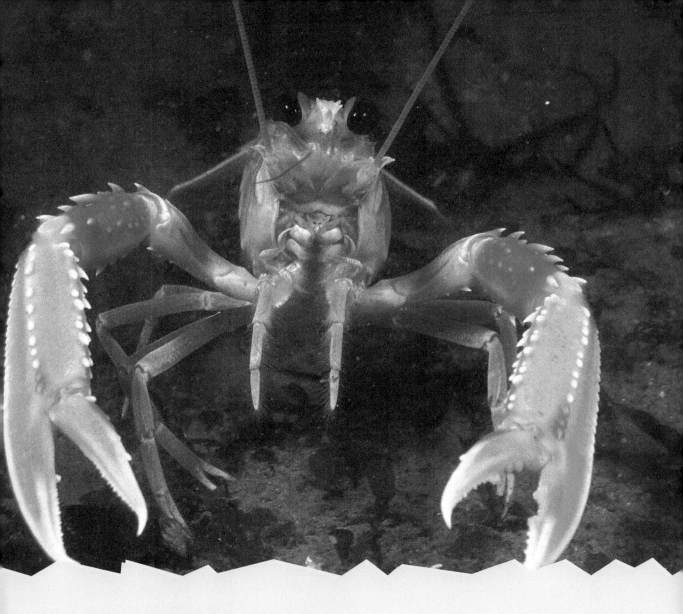

A lobster grows and changes.

A lobster needs air and **sunlight**.

A lobster is **living**.

Is a Rock Living or Nonliving?

A rock does not need food or water.

A rock does not move on its own.

A rock does not grow and change on its own.

A rock does not need air or **sunlight**.

A rock is **nonliving**.

Is a Fish Living or Nonliving?

A fish grows and changes.

A fish needs food and water.

A fish moves on its own.

A fish needs air and **sunlight**.

A fish is **living**.

Is Sand Living or Nonliving?

Sand does not move on its own.

Sand does not need food or water.

Sand does not grow on its own.

Sand does not need air or **sunlight**.

Sand is **nonliving**.

Is a Dolphin Living or Nonliving?

A dolphin grows and changes.

A dolphin needs food and water.

A dolphin moves on its own.

A dolphin needs air and **sunlight**.

A dolphin is **living**.

Is Seaweed Living or Nonliving?

Seaweed moves on its own toward the sun.

Seaweed gets food from the sun.

Seaweed grows and changes.

Seaweed needs air and **sunlight**.

Seaweed is **living**.

What Do You Think?

Is this iceberg **living** or **nonliving**?

Glossary

living alive. Living things need food and water. They breathe and move on their own. They grow and change.

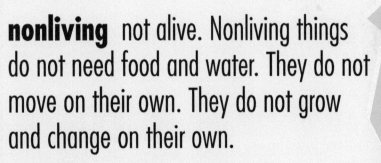

lobster animal that lives in the ocean. It has a hard shell and big claws.

nonliving not alive. Nonliving things do not need food and water. They do not move on their own. They do not grow and change on their own.

sunlight light from the sun

Find Out More

Websites

Facthound offers a safe, fun way to find Internet sites related to this book. All of the sites on Facthound have been researched by our staff.

Here's all you do:
Visit www.facthound.com
Type in this code: 9781410953810

Books

Lindeen, Carol K. *Living and Nonliving.* Mankato, Minn.: Capstone, 2008.

Llewellyn, Claire. *Oceans (Habitat Survival).* Chicago: Raintree, 2013.

Scott, Janine. *An Ocean of Animals (Habitats Around the World).* Mankato, Minn.: Capstone, 2012.

Index